Hounds on the Mountain

Hounds on the Mountain

POEMS

James Still

**FIRESIDE
INDUSTRIES**

1937 edition published by Viking

2022 edition published by Fireside Industries
An imprint of the University Press of Kentucky

Copyright © 2022 by The University Press of Kentucky

Editorial and Sales Offices: The University Press of Kentucky
663 South Limestone Street, Lexington, Kentucky 40508-4008
www.kentuckypress.com

Cataloging-in-Publication Data for the 1937 edition is available at the Library of
Congress.

ISBN 978-1-950564-22-4 (pbk. : alk. paper)
ISBN 978-1-950564-23-1 (pdf)
ISBN 978-1-950564-24-8 (epub)

This book is printed on acid-free paper meeting
the requirements of the American National Standard
for Permanence in Paper for Printed Library Materials.

Manufactured in the United States of America.

Illustrations by Aurora Noctua.

To G. L. and Jethro

Contents

IV. Death on the Mountain

V. The Hill-Born

I
Hounds on the Mountain

Child in the Hills

Where on these hills are tracks a small foot made,
Where rests the echo of his voice calling to the crows
In sprouting corn? Here are tall trees his eyes
Have measured to their tops, here lies fallow earth
Unfurrowed by terracing plows these sleeping years.
Here flow the waters of Carr before his darkened door.

I cannot see you, child, but I can hear your voice
Shrill and imperious with rain in the beechwood trees.
In the dark hours I have heard your questing words
Creep out of nowhere in the mountain silence;
I have heard your small heart beat with low whispering
In measured breaths of deep night, ebbing and returning.

                        Now you are shod against the earth.
Once your eager toes were thrust with gladness in the soil
And smooth pebbles welled between your willing toes;
Once you waded the clear stony waters of Carr
And perch fled before your steps in swaying silver zigzags.

Once, waking in the night, open-eyed and wondering
You heard geese flying over, and you listened, breathless;
Once swift feet of horses echoed when your brother died,
Once the waters of Carr rose in the night to flooding
And you heard the swelling voice of the water's strength.

Now you have fled with the geese, with the hoofs at midnight,
Swept with the waters down the winding mountain valleys,
Drifted into years of growth and strange enmeshment,
But the child did not go. . . .

He is waiting under the shadow of these hills.
In the damp coolness of laurel and rhododendron;
He is lost in the mossy coves, in the lynn's late sighing.
His voice is drowned in the waters of Carr.

Mountain Dulcimer

The dulcimer sings from fretted maple throat
Of the doe's swift poise, the fox's fleeting step
And music of hounds upon the outward slope
Stirring the night, drumming the ridge-strewn way,
The anvil's strength . . .
                    and the silence after
That aches and cries unhushed into the day.

From the dulcimer's breast sound hunting horns
Strong as clenched hands upon the edge of death,
The creak of saddle-bags, of oxen yoke and thongs,
Wild turkey's treble, dark sudden flight of crows,
Of unshod hoofs . . .
                    and the stillness after,
Bitter as salt drenching the tongue of pain:

And of the lambs crying, breath of the lark,
Long drinks from piggins hard against the lips;
And with hoarse singing, raw as hickory shagbark,
The foal's anxiety is woven with the straining wedge
And the wasp's anger . . .
                    and the quiet after
For the carver of maple on a keen blade's edge.

Fox Hunt

Fox in the thorn-patch . . .

Shrill notes of a sheep's horn billow down the hills
Crusted with shadows. Fetch the long rifle from the wall,
Draw ramrod and tallow-dipped rag through the slender shaft,
Awakening a dulled skill. Bring out the rusty bullet mold
With a finger of lead; blow a slow fire upon the cold hearth.
Shave the lead pellets to a good roundness ere the wildcat
Chills the night with his crying.

Call up the yawning hounds from the chimney's warmth
Beneath the puncheon floor. Call up the dusty hounds
With a rasher of sow-belly and a greasy corn-pone
While fog loiters in the valleys and dark coves
Over blossoming elder and wine-red sumac,
And a swollen moon rides the sky-orchards.

Bright on the mountain the hunter's fire strips darkness down
From quavering poplars fluting the night;
And slouched shadows wall the glow against a taller sky
Listening through the leaf-sounds. Listening:

The hills muffle the long crying, then suddenly clear
Over razor-back ridges comes a wild freshet of barking.

Hounds flow down the slope in a narrowing sweep
And up again in brown tidal strokes.
Their voices are the wild trumpets
Catching the night air for their blasting:

Thin, high-nasal, the young hounds with soft brown eyes
Burst into a stark tenor. Thunderous and earthy,
The bass-viol music of old hounds rends the damp air.

Gaunt and anxious the swiftening pace
Flings the dogs clamoring down the trail
Where an odd prescience guiding padded feet shall fail
And a gum-stump mark the end of a perilous way.

In the stern interval when warm blood stains the earth
And the mellow banjos of the hounds' throats are still,
A catamount cries the chilled and living day.

Horse Swapping on Troublesome Creek

Splintery as legs of spring foals the willows bend
Over Troublesome's sudden banks hemming drifts of sand
Against slow thin water, against the mare's stiff heels
Wheeling in the dry creek bed with casual step;
And the sun-pierced shade of willows settles unsteadily
Among the throng of stallions champing their bits
And straining new leather with arrogant heads.

High in their polished saddles the traders ride
With stinging lash and blunt spur deep against the side
Of goaded pony, of anxious filly swinging heavily,
Of spavined mare plucking heels with sharp precision
From bedding sand. Combed, curried and clipped
Their smooth breasts glisten and long muscular necks
Rise clean and springy into tight bridles.

The traders measure with keen practiced glance
The height from withers to croup, feel trembling flesh,
Rub hard careless hands over quivering muscles
And peer coldly into moist sad eyes.
Only the foals toss unbound heads
With flash of hock and unsheared flowing manes,
Flexing clumsy legs in short unhindered quests
Down the aisles of sand to the hill's uplifted girth.
An untamed heart is swift upon the earth.

Infare

He was the sun-bronzed, resolute and free,
Who buckled his belt against the universe
And challenged the taut rope of mortality:
She, the sweet apples from high green orchards,
The faint grey line of day within a purple land,
The slender willow, the sudden piping voice,
A crystal from the flint-beds of the coves
Whose strength lay in the wildness of her choice.

The calloused hand that grasped the fragile one
Was burning daylight to a feeble star,
A smoking jut of mountains near the sun.

There were busy fiddles and elderberry wine,
And clumsy feet striking the boarded floor
With jarring notes that rimmed the flowing night.
There the ashy face and faded rheumy eye
Blushed and sparkled in the tallow light.

They fled outside beneath the walnut trees
Where a dead-white moon was roistering,
Drawing its beams in skeins across the shadow seas.
His eyes turned back against the wooded ridge

With lonesome glance upon youth withdrawn;
Her heart was quick to climb with breathless sigh
To blossoming orchards of familiar peace.
And mountains laid cold heads against the sky.

When the Dulcimers Are Gone

When the dulcimers are mingled with the dust
Of flowering chestnut, and their lean fretted necks
Are slain maple stalks, their strings dull threads of rust,
Where shall the mellow voice be heard upon the hills,
Upon what pennyroyal meadow, beside what rills?

Where shall the gentle words in mild abandon sing
With sweet design in loitering melody
As flights of swallows aimless on the wing,
Yet skilled as scythes that curve through yellow grain
And fragrant as jasmine after freshening rain?

Or may the heart's breath on the slender reed
Sing bright virelays to match the oriole?—
The tulip tree the lyre that one must heed
When the dulcimers are gone, when afternoons attend
The silver underleaf of poplars in the wind?

Journey beyond the Hills

The wind-drawn manes
And supple knees of the stallions fly the gate
Of hills to smooth meadows beyond the mountain wall;
And the strong mares drink in quivering haste
From the limestone waters, turning their anxious heads
Toward greener shores of grass, toward clattering passings
Of the fleet and proud.
                           Down the mountain lanes,
Down the heavy-hipped ridges stricken and unforested,
They have gone with the streams unhalted and draining
The narrow valleys of the flesh of earth.

O slow the hand and fleet the hoof upon the mountainside
Where men within their prisoning hills have stayed.
Swift are their hearts upon this journey never made.

Hounds on the Mountain

Slow the dull fulcrum, slow the arched leanings
Of hill on hill and witless lifting of stark eyes
To craven stone. White the wet lattice of morning
Over dusty drums, and keen the agony of dry roots
Questing beneath the earth.
                              Lean as brown straws
The hounds of day tread out thickets of darkness,
Damp the grasses their bodies have brushed in passing,
Thinner than fly-wings, heavier than words in a cavern,
Wilder than thoughts creaming the tongue unspoken.

Hounds on the mountain . . .
Grey and swift spinning the quarry shall turn
At the cove's ending, at the slow day's breaking,
And lave the violent shadows with her blood.

II

Creek Country

On Troublesome Creek

These people here were born for mottled hills,
The narrow trails, the creek-bed roads
Quilting dark ridges and pennyroyal valleys.
Where Troublesome gathers forked waters
Into one strong body they have come down
To push the hills away, to shape sawn timbers
Into homeseats, to heap firm stones into chimneys,
And rear their young before splendid fires.

And Troublesome floods with spring's dark waters,
Dries to sand in summer, and purple martins
Flock to poled gourds, molting stained feathers
Which fall like blackened snow on clapboard roofs
Of hill townsmen biding eternal time.
And men here wait as mountains long have waited.

On Redbird Creek

Now all of earth that fills the valley's breast
Is turned in furrows and the ram's horn rots
Where cloven soil has penned the acres up
With greenness prim and ordered into lots.
And all of oak and lynn that strode the west
Of Redbird Creek where crows and blackbirds call
Are things of mist grown stark and tall.

The vibrant canes crowding marshy ground
Are tuneless pipes heard by bleeding ears
Through blighted chestnut cankered to the heart
And rousing all of memory's ancient fears.
These foils of clouds that men and plows attend
Are tares and thistles strewn upon the wind.

Farm

In the deep moist hollows, on the burnt acres
Suspended upon the mountainside, the crisp green corn
Tapers blunt to the fruiting tassel;
Long straight shafts of yellow poplar
Strike upward like prongs of lightning at the field's edge,
Dwarfing the tender blades, the jointed growth;
Crows haggle their dark feathers, glare beady eyes
Surveying the slanted crop from the poplar boughs,
Opening purple beaks to cry the ripening feast,
And flow from their perch in heavy pointless flight.
A lizard, timid and tremulous, swallowing clots of air
With pulsing throat, pauses at the smooth trunk
And runs up the sky with liquid feet.

Spring on Troublesome Creek

Not all of us were warm, not all of us.
We are winter-lean, our faces are sharp with cold
And there is a smell of wood smoke in our clothes;
Not all of us were warm, though we hugged the fire
Through the long chilled nights.

                                 We have come out
Into the sun again, we have untied our knot
Of flesh: We are no thinner than a hound or mare,
Or an unleaved poplar. We have come through
To the grass, to the cows calving in the lot.

Court Day

They have come early into the town.
Dark as plowed earth the rising and the setting out
On the creek-bed road, down the stony waters of Troublesome,
Down the cold thin flowing, willow-dark and waking.
They have come early to Justice, following the water's sound
Out of the beechwood hollows.

Why the dark journey? Was the landmark moved?
Perhaps it walked alone, wanting to stir itself
And rest slantwise upon another place.
Will Justice gladden your summer's plowing?

The jury sits upon the bench.
The judge sleeps in his chair, and the noon-bright hills
Crowd the tall windows, spreading their enormous curtain
Against the light's pouring, heat-waved and burning.
They have sat long upon the bench, with Justice droning
Out of a hornet's throat.

Do not indict me. Let me shake your hand.
If the landmark wanders I shall take your part.
My testimony is sound. I swear by the hills,
By these eternal landmarks of the heart.

On Double Creek

I was born on Double Creek, on a forty-acre hill.
North was the Buckalew Ridge, south at our land's end
The county poor farm with hungry fields
And furrows as crooked as an adder's track.

Across the creek I saw the paupers plowing.
I can remember their plodding in the furrows,
Their palsied hands, the worn flesh of their faces,
And their odd shapelessness, and their tired cries.
I can remember the dark swift martins in their eyes.

III
Earth-Bread

Mountain Coal Town

These stark houses hung upon the hills,
The ragged slopes and interstices of the barren rock
Are havens for miners in an upper world.
Here is their pool of daylight and their stars
Waiting after darkness in the gutted cave
Emersed in coal and slate and flickering gleam.
A sweeter dampness rises from the river's flowing
Than leaks from the black caverns of the earth,
And the ear here turns to man's firm laughter
And the long clear whistle of the cardinal singing.

Earth-Bread

Under stars cool as the copperhead's eyes,
Under hill-horizons cut clean and deft with wind,
Beneath this surface night, below earth and rock,
The picks strike into veins of coal, oily and rich
And centuries-damp.

They dig with short heavy strokes, straining shoulders
Practiced and bulging with labor,
Crumbling the marrow between the shelving slate,
Breaking the hard, slow-yielding seams.
Bent into flesh-knots the miners dig this earth-bread,
This stone-meat, these fruited bones.

This is the eight-hour death, the daily burial
In a dark harvest lost as any dead,

Night in the Coal Camps

Cold yellow windows to the night, the trees
Frozen with dark, and eyes sleepless
Along rutted streets. Clear the sparrow words
Pierce thumb-latched doors; blowing they pass
Like field larks dustily through seeding grass.

Drawn faces on pillows, mouths hollowed in breathing
The unquiet air; and the million-tongued night tremulous
With crickets' rasping thighs, with sharp cluckings
Of fowls under drafty floors. In the caverns deep
The picks strike into coal and slate. They do not sleep.

IV
Death on the Mountain

Pattern for Death

The spider puzzles his legs and rests his web
On aftergrass. No winds stir here to break
The quiet design, nothing protests the weaving
Of taut threads in a ladder of silk:
He is clever, he is fastidious, and intricate;
He is skilled with his cords of hate.

Who can escape through the grass? The crane-fly
Quivers its body in paralytic sleep;
The giant moths shed their golden dust
From fettered wings, and the spider speeds his lust.

Who reads the language of direction? Where may we pass
Through the immense pattern sheer as glass?

Death on the Mountain

I
No child he had
Nor any kin,
Only the cold
January wind
To speak the hopeful word
At death:

Two hound dogs
To cry his dirge,
And Troublesome's tide
To sweep and surge
Over fevered brain
At death.

Only a fiddle
Beside his bed
Brightening his days
Before life fled.
Only remembered song
At death.

II
Ewes' first wool and linsey cloth
Shall line the grave box for this child,
And smooth-grained chestnut sawn and planed
Be his wooden garment for a while.

The earth shall rise up where he lies
With steady reach, and permanent.
A shroud of cedars be his mound,
This shield of hills his monument.

III
And Troublesome's dead are quartered with the roots
That split firm stone and suck the marrow out,
And finger yellowing bones that lie astray,
Free from design, released from life, from death
And all of light and darkness, and the disarray
Of pathways in a brush-choked wood.
Only the hills are marked where they have stood.

Graveyard

Nothing has moved in this town.
Nothing at all. Only the soundless dark
And the wonder of night that came like wind
Unseen have wandered down these final streets.
Only the silent have come upon this mark.

There is no town so quiet on any earth,
Nor any house so dark upon the mind.
Only the night is here, and the dead
Under the hard blind eyes of hill and tree.
Here lives sleep. Here the dead are free.

Epitaph for Uncle Ira Combs, Mountain Preacher

So long on mountains he had looked,
All earth was dull that did not tower up
Into the sky.
          So long upon the hills
Of faith his soul had calmly leaned,
He was a bulwark firm within his God,
A mountain rising high.

Nixie Middleton

I am alone and all the hills have eyed my sorrow,
And bird and fox have heard my breath along the slopes
Whistling your name. I have searched the brief green hollows
Of Honey Gap, of Seven Lynn and the cool beechwood cove
Of Dead Mare Branch, calling you down from every hill,
Calling my love. There were the hermit cries
Of birds that pricked the leaves and fell on spears of moss;
In Flaxpatch Hollow a mourning dove sang through the knobs
His sad young song, his *a-coo-o, coo-o, coo-o,*
With his mate lost and all his sorrow true.

I have gone up the lonesome valley where the whippoorwill
Sings his dark speech; up Sand Lick, up Carr's clear waters
And the sixty-seven mile wandering of Troublesome Creek.
I have gone up to the graveyard on a laurel-thicket hill
Where my love sleeps. My love waits for me still.

Death in the Forest

I was born humble. At the foot of mountains
My face was set upon the immensity of earth
And stone; and upon oaks full-bodied and old.
There is so much writ upon the parchment of leaves,
So much of beauty blown upon the winds,
I can but fold my hands and sink my knees
In the leaf-pages. Under the mute trees
I have cried with this scattering of knowledge,
Beneath the flight of birds shaken with this waste
Of wings.
       I was born humble. My heart grieves
Beneath this wealth of wisdom perished with the leaves.

Come Down from the Hills

And here again to the flight of leaves and birds
Through sky-space and the dusty stickweed bonnets;
Here to the pawpaw thickets lush with frosted fruit,
To the hills new in their silent wintering,
And the clean white mantle of snow new-fallen.

Come down from the hills when the days curl
Into early dark, when hours crowd the thick door
And slip through sill cracks to the bitter air;
Come when the hollowed ice has claimed the grass
And blown its breath across the haggard months.

The fox has writ its passage on the frozen ridge,
The crows their feedings in the glassy sedge,
And iced white wings of death stalk in the coves.
Come down from the hills. O never know
The stark thawing agony of blood on snow.

Passenger Pigeons

Here was a symphony of wings,
An aerial river of birds across the sky in thunderous floods
Of slate-blue feathers, a host of violet throats
Splitting the sky with one unerring thrust.

Here were red feet of pigeons spilling
Like blood through the trees, breaking the forest down
In their dense roosting wild with guttural cooing.
Here in this weight of wings were folded death and dust.

V
The Hill-Born

The Hill-Born

They have come down astride their bony nags
In the gaunt hours when the lean young day
Walks the grey ridge, and cool light flags
Smooth-bodied poplars piercing a hollow sky.
They have come forth against the day's down-curving
From wall-darkened beds where a child's breathing
Flows beyond measure with the crickets' chirping,
Or cicadas' song in seventeenth year spawning,
Greeting the earth before the leprous mist
Melts in the sun's bronze weaving.

They are uprisen with the strong and fleet
Whose footsteps weave no trace in aftergrass,
Forth with broadax and with adz and fro
Where forests edge the ancient wilderness,
To hew and flay among the patriarchs
And bring their strength and agèd glory low.

Upon broad hills their scythes are swinging,
In the high fields severing vine and stalk,
The blade's arched stroke is wildly singing
A song echoing from earth's dull throat.
A sweep of years will bring them all to lie
Wrapped in strange flowering of earth and sky.

Starveling trees bear so sweet a fruit
Along the shallow amblings of Squabble Creek,
Down the prisoned waters of Troublesome:

Spring tides surging to the naked root
Have carved a road for wheel and hoof,
And writ their passage on the living rock.

Down the broad hills earth-born lays are sung,
Sweet as a lark's song whispered down the wind—
Never the free shall know a stricken tongue.

White Highways

I have gone out to the roads that go up and down
In smooth white lines, stoneless and hard;
I have seen distances shortened between two points,
The hills pushed back and bridges thrust across
The shallow river's span.

To the broad highways, and back again I have come
To the creek-bed roads and narrow winding trails
Worn into ruts by hoofs and steady feet;
I have come back to the long way around,
The far between, the slow arrival.
Here is my pleasure most where I have lived
And called my home.
                    O do not wander far
From the rooftree and the hill-gathered earth;
Go not upon these wayfares measured with a line
Drawn hard and white from birth to death.
O quiet and slow is peace, and curved with space
Brought back again to this warm homing place.

Rain on the Cumberlands

Through the stricken air, through the buttonwood balls
Suspended on twig-strings, the rain fog circles and swallows,
Climbs the shallow plates of bark, the grooved trunks,
And wind-pellets go hurrying through the leaves.
Down, down the rain; down in plunging streaks
Of watered grey.

Rain in the beechwood trees. Rain upon the wanderer
Whose breath lies cold upon the mountainside,
Caught up with broken horns within the nettled grass,
With hoofs relinquished on the breathing stones
Eaten with rain-strokes.

Rain has buried her seed and her dead.
They spring together in this fertile air
Loud with thunder.

Uncle Ambrose

Your hair is growing long, Uncle Ambrose,
And the strands of your beard are like willow sprays
Hanging over Troublesome Creek's breeze in August.
Uncle Ambrose, your hands are heavy with years,
Seamy with the ax's heft, the plow's hewn stock,
The thorn wound and the stump-dark bruise of time.

Your face is a map of Knott County
With hard ridges of flesh, the wrinkled creek beds,
The traces and forks carved like wagon tracks on stone;
And there is Troublesome's valley struck violently
By a barlow's blade, and the anti-cline of all waters
This side of the Kentucky River.

Your teeth are dark-stained apples on an ancient tree
And your eyes the trout pools between the narrow hills;
Your hands are glacial drifts of stone
Cradled on a mountain top:
One is Big Ball Mountain, rock-ribbed and firm,
One the Appalachian range from Maine to Alabama.

Eyes in the Grass

A rusty grackle walks the apple's bough.
He wanders through a green cloth of leaves
With back arched impudently, and pauses,
Plump-bodied and balanced, searching beneath.

There are eyes in the grass,
Eyes lying still beneath stalk and pod where doodles
Drill their earthen cones, and ants march in a forest
Of living swords.

I think that neither the grackle's black eyes
Nor the ant's myopic sight has found me here,
Drowned in quivering stems, lost in wattled twigs
Of grass-trees. Oh, I am lost to any wandering view.
I am a hill uncharted, my breathing is the wind.
I am horizon. I am earth's far end.

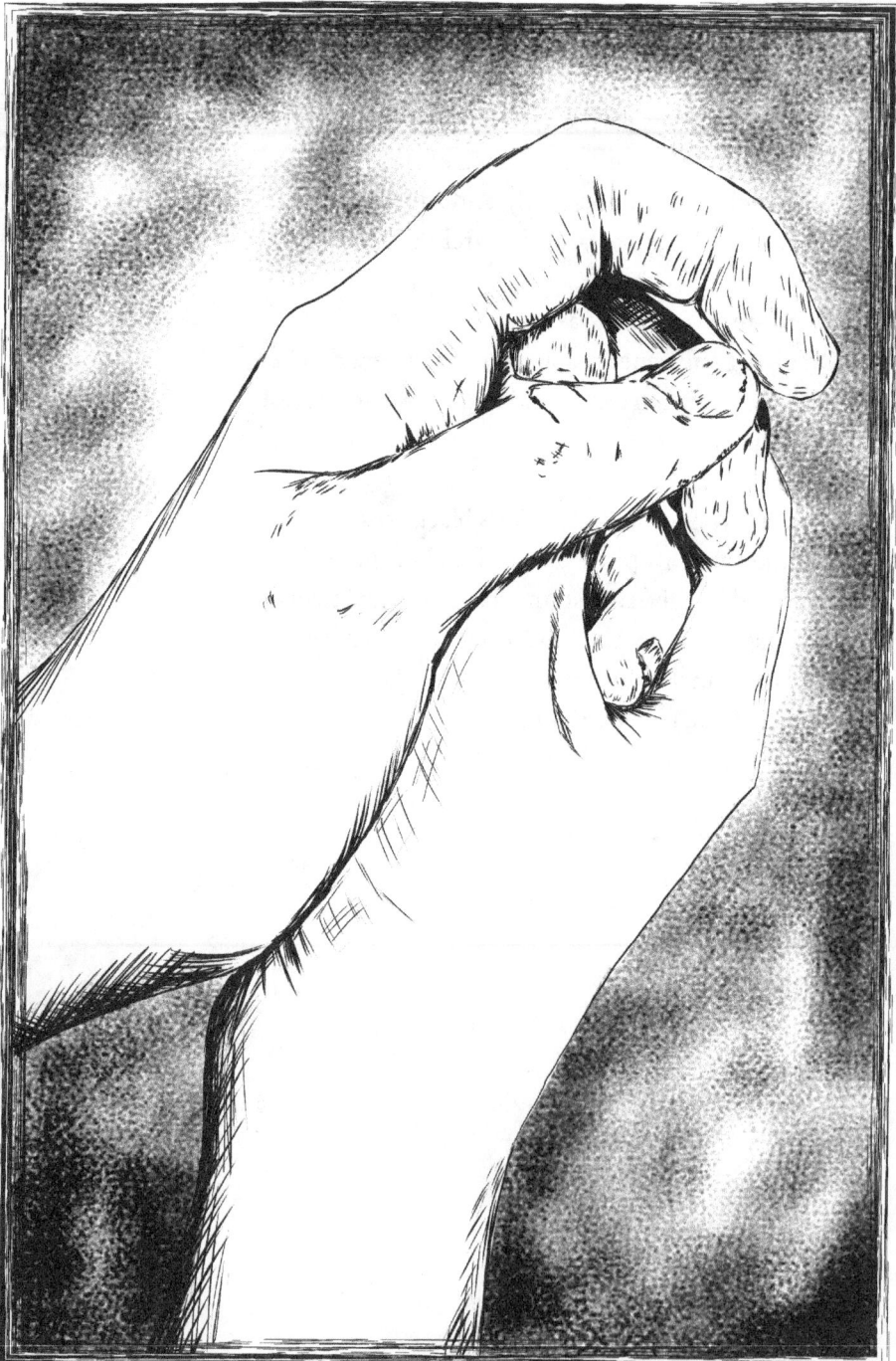

With Hands Like Leaves

The hounds sleep well. It is not they who stir the fox
And fret the owl; it is I, wandering on quiet feet.
It is I upon this high land sharpened by the moon.
I have gone softly, I have seen small eyes burn white
In thicket-dark, and I have heard sleep-twitters sound
Where the mulberry sheds its caterpillar fruit.

This is not a mountain I walk upon. It is a ridge
Of sleep or death, a slope hung on a night-jar's speech.
A child walks here with hands like leaves, with eyes
Like swifts that search the darkness in a perilous land.
He seeks a hill where living day shall stand.

On Buckhorn Creek

Under the grackle's words, under the hard bead
Of the crow's eyes, the foal is dropped, the furrows laid
With a new excellence, and the seed-roots grasp the clod
Through leafrib and the rotted weed.

These are the acres served with love and plow
Through drought and thaw and rain's re-ordering;
This is a land down-leaning toward the wind
And terraced with wisdom from the cowbird's tongue.

On dark acres of the mind no bird's throat cries
The winter's growing, the germinal leaf that dies.

Year of the Pigeons

In the year of the passenger pigeons
They came in a darkening flood, and the valley of Troublesome
Was heavy with sound. The soft gutturals of their cooing
Were harrows that raked the air and drowned the locusts' thighs.
They came with a cloud of wings that thundered down the hills
And broke the forest with their weight of flesh. Here fell
A snow of dung, here oak and lynn were shaggy with their nests;
Here field and wood, the grain and stalk lost in a feathered hell.

The hollows of Troublesome Creek were glutted with pigeons.
They blew like wind through the trees, and the shuck-dry leaves
Flew from their scratching on the molding floor.
These were no crows flapping above a cornfield:
This was a fire that ran through patch and brush
Eating the milky nubbins, the tender shoots,
The leaf-hoppers, the cankerworms, and maggots of crane-flies
At the grass roots.

The red agate of the pigeons' eyes was the color of death—
Death quiet upon a nest, death feeding her curious milk
From bulging crop, death hovering over pin-feathered squab
With whole-eyed glance upon an infertile egg
On twig-lined shelf: the male warming the oval bulb
Between his legs, squatting with drooping wings;
The female taking her turn upon this stubborn fruit
Of their mating. Death was the silence in the stricken yolk
Turning a living semblance to the trusting breast;
Death running with blood-red feet, with wind-bright eyes
Where wing is interleaved with wing and nest with nest.

Come to the hills! Come to the pigeon roost for plentiful flesh.
Come with clap nets, O come with hawk and buzzard to this feast
Upon the breasts of heaven. Prowl with the skunk and fox
To sever these soft throats; light up the stinking sulphur pots
In the night forest. O come with death's long flail and pole
For this ripe manna. Empty the tree-cotes of their fledglings,
And pile and gather and carry away a dying windfall harvest
With blood-beads hardened in a thousand beaks.

Now have the pigeons perished, the flocking millions slain,
And all the quiet red eyes become a single glance of dust
Blown through the beechwood coves. Now has the winter's rain
Swept down the simple nests, and now the boughs are still—
Flesh, wing and eye devoured, a countless horde brought low
And not a slate-blue feather blows on any hill.

Horseback in the Rain

With rain in the face
And leathern thongs moist
In the hands, where halt
The mud-scattered journey
For the crust, the salt
Of bread upon the tongue?

Where turn from the flow
Of day slanted greyly
Toward earth, toward the dark
Shaken upon this rank of hills?
Where turn for the spark
Of eyes burnt warmly?

To the stone, to the mud
With hoofs busy clattering
In a fog-wrinkled spreading
Of waters? Halt not. Stay not.
Ride the storm with no ending
On a road unarriving.

Heritage

I shall not leave these prisoning hills
Though they topple their barren heads to level earth
And the forests slide uprooted out of the sky.
Though the waters of Troublesome, of Trace Fork,
Of Sand Lick rise in a single body to glean the valleys,
To drown lush pennyroyal, to unravel rail fences;
Though the sun-ball breaks the ridges into dust
And burns its strength into the blistered rock
I cannot leave. I cannot go away.

Being of these hills, being one with the fox
Stealing into the shadows, one with the new-born foal,
The lumbering ox drawing green beech logs to mill,
One with the destined feet of man climbing and descending,
And one with death rising to bloom again, I cannot go.
Being of these hills I cannot pass beyond.